The Playbook to Success

By
Dr. Rudolph A. Moseley, Jr.

TABLE OF CONTENTS

Recommendations and Endorsements

"*The Playbook to Success* serves as a guide and an inspiration for young black men to achieve success despite what people may say about them. Dr. Moseley articulates the attributes needed to attain success. This is a must-read book."

Philip N. Miller, PhD. --retired professor and chair, Department of Engineering and Technology, Community College of Rhode Island

Co-Pastor Shekinah, Family Worship Center Providence, Rhode Island

"As an educator who has worked with students for over 30 years, it is rare to find a book that speaks directly to those often-overlooked traits needed for success. There is much more that is required for true success other than hard work and determination. Tremendously successful persons possess many of the important character traits spoken of in *The Playbook to Success*. In this book, Dr. Moseley has pulled back the curtain to reveal many attributes that are overlooked but are key to opening doors of opportunity. Our youth need to know how to "jostle," how to "navigate" and how to discover their "X-factor" – all addressed by Dr. Moseley in this eye-opening book. No young person in the game of being the best that they can, should be without this essential playbook."

Shawn Turnquest, B.Ed., MA
School Administrator
Nassau, Bahamas

"As a student of Meta-physics, religions and modern philosophies, I am intrigued that Dr. Rudolph Moseley, Jr's book, *The Playbook to Success,* in clear and direct presentation, highlights and guides the reader toward action steps necessary to manifest success in all areas of life and living."

Rodney D. Smith. Ed.D.
President and CEO,
University of The Bahamas

"Dr Rudolph Moseley's book, *The Playbook to Success,* is one of the most inspirational books I have ever read. I recommend everybody desiring to make a difference in life to read it. This book will help you ignite the passion and desire to reach your God intended purpose and destiny in your life."

Bishop Adams Lwesya

National Overseer

Malawi Pentecostal H. Association Church

Malawi, Africa

"Dr. Rudolph Moseley Jr, is uniquely qualified to instruct and inspire the generations on how to create a plan and consistently pray, work, study and overcome every challenge in order to lay a foundation and establish a Playbook for the world to follow!!!"

Pastor Matthew K Thompson

Jubilee Christian Church

Boston, MA

"*The Playbook to Success* is an engaging and much-needed guide to help high school teens navigate today's complex world of choices and distractions. An entrepreneur, educator, and former athlete, Dr. Rudolph Moseley, Jr. offers a practical approach for adapting to pivotal behaviors and understanding the power of positive self-talk. It is chock-full of personal anecdotes, and offers a road map as well as some tried-and-true principles to help today's youth achieve success. "

Opal Gayle

High School Teacher

Fall River, MA, USA

Dear Dr. Rudy Moseley

"Your path to complete success began with your love of and surrender to the lordship of Christ. Your growth was strengthened by the wisdom of humility: the understanding that without God, nothing of eternal value or benefit is possible. This truth saddled you with a determination to discipline yourself to live a holy life of love, honesty, education, and achievement for the selfless benefit of others. You my son, have reached the spiritual maturity of being grounded for the distinct purpose of being a man who is a blessing; "...like a tree planted by streams of water, which yields its fruit in season and whose leaf does not wither. Whatever he does (you do) prospers." (Psa. 1:3 parentheses mine) Yvonne and I are blessed to be part of you and Latoya's life.

Bishop Gideon Thompson

Founder Jubilee Christian Church

Boston, MA

Good Afternoon Dr. Moseley,

You may not remember me but I was a student at Hope High when you were the principal. I was in your office almost everyday to a point where you would see me in the office and just tell me to sit there until change of period. It took me some time but looking back at it, you could've discouraged me from being a better student, you could've suspended me from always being in your office but instead you did the opposite. Although you were sick of seeing my face, you were always positive with me. I just wanted to take the time to say thank you for that. I've grown so much and guys like you played an important role in my development.

Thank you for being tough on me but also for knowing when to give me tough love. Hope all is well with you and yours and Happy New Year!

Jordan Maddox, Master of Science
Former Student, USA

DEDICATION

This book is dedicated to my wonderful wife Latoya and our 6
amazing sons Jaden, Jalen, Jace, Justin (late), Justus and Baby Jay.
I have learned so much from each of your lives. I thank God for
the opportunity to be your father.

Acknowledgments

I thank my son Jaden Moseley for the book title. I thank my son Jalen Moseley for the front cover picture. I thank my parents Rudolph Moseley Sr and Patricia Moseley for life and for being a great example of what to strive for. Thank you for your leadership and support as you not only set the standard but gave me and my siblings the opportunity to meet and exceed the bar. I love you both with all my heart.

I also want to thank my BOL family. You all have been an amazing congregation. Thank you for giving my wife and I the opportunity to be your shepherd.

I also thank my Lord and Savior Jesus Christ for saving my life and giving me purpose."

Excerpt From: Dr. Rudolph A. Moseley, Jr. "The Playbook to Success." Apple Books.

PREFACE

Only one percent of the world's population has a PhD. Less than one percent is Black, and less than that is male. When I was young I told my parents that I wanted to be a doctor. I had a dream very early on before I knew the road that I would have to travel, the mountains I would have to climb, or the obstacles that I would have to overcome. My dream was to make a difference in this world by helping others. In any event I made it. I achieved what many desire to achieve but very few attain. I decided to write this book to inspire the younger me. I can remember that although I had big dreams, one of my main obstacles was that I struggled as a reader. I struggled in school for many years but still focused on pushing forward. It is my hope that as a student, this book will help you develop the winning mindset and the habits to be successful. As a young Black man in America who has achieved a desired level of academic and professional success, with advanced degrees, married to the same woman for over twenty years, and having children with only that woman, I know that unfortunately, I am very rare. I wanted to show especially other young black men that you can also achieve success despite what people may say about you. People's opinions of you do not dictate who you are nor do they give you your value. You are valuable because God made you valuable.

Chapter 1: Attitude

The greatest discovery of all time is that a person can change his future by merely changing his attitude.

— *Oprah Winfrey.*

Attitude *(noun)*

A settled way of thinking or feeling about someone or something, typically one that is reflected in a person's behavior.

my self-talk.

She took a tough attitude toward other people's indulgences.

It is often said that your attitude determines your altitude. Mahatma Gandhi wrote: "Keep your thoughts positive because your thoughts become your words, keep your words positive because your words become your behavior, keep your behavior positive because your behavior becomes your habits, keep your habits positive because your habits become your values, keep your values positive because your values become your destiny."

I always believed that I was going to be great and was going to do great things. However, what I did not know were the steps that would lead me to greatness. Step one, cultivate the right attitude as this is the foundation upon which all actions are based.

I once read that if you don't like something, change it. If you can't change it, change your attitude about it. When it comes to academic success and academic performance your attitude is the greatest asset to ensure academic success. You must believe that you can achieve it. You must believe that you can conquer it. You must believe that you can overcome it. You must believe that no matter how difficult an obstacle or a task might be, that you can master it. The label of being smart is something that is often overrated because being smart is one person's opinion or their label given based on how well you can perform at a particular task.

There is a saying that is widely thought/believed: "that practice makes perfect." I strongly disagree with this statement. I believe instead that practice makes improvement. When I think about my life, one of the obstacles that I had to overcome was having a negative attitude when faced with difficult circumstances. In college, at the University of Nebraska-Lincoln, I was a track and field athlete. I was a sprinter and a long jumper. We practiced for many hours. The purpose of the practices was to help us improve by making us better, faster, stronger. Often in practice, we had to run many 200-meter dashes and at a particular pace. I never liked that particular workout because of the pain that was associated with it. I would be in incredible pain and at the end of the workout, I was overcome by feelings of exhaustion. My butt muscles would be sore, and at the end of each run I would collapse on the track and wonder, "why am I doing this to myself?" Nevertheless, I would get up and get back to the next run or return to practice the next day. I did not enjoy the workout but I did like what it produced in me - I became faster. I apply this same principle to academics. I love the fact that I have a doctoral degree. I love the fact that I have a master's degree. I love the fact that I have a bachelor's degree. I love the gratification that I felt to walk across that stage to make my parents and my family proud. The satisfaction of making those that looked up to me feel proud was priceless. To accomplish the goals I had for myself, I had to change my thinking and my approach to difficult assignments especially in the area of reading. I had to change my attitude towards reading. And, eventually accepted that reading was not a bad thing. Reading was something that I had to get good at if I wanted to get the things I wanted out of life.

I think back to my early struggles with reading early on in my life ... Attitude is all about how you think about something, and how you approach it. Attitude is a means to an end. I have come to realize that to be a leader you must be a reader. I also realized that I could not get to my next level without doing some of the things that I might not like or enjoy. So my attitude had to change. Attitude is extremely important when it comes to academic achievement because not everything is going to come easy and just because something is hard doesn't mean that it's impossible. My attitude is basically what I think about something. I have to change the way I approach difficult situations and not run from them. I have to focus on what is good, what is praiseworthy, what is the benefit of this activity to my future goals. I have to think about these things and say "I can do this." I can achieve at a high-level. I can overcome this obstacle. I can pass this class.

We have to change the language of our self-talk. To do this, we have to first change our thinking, then, we have to change our language, and then we have to change our actions. Once we change our actions, we will be able to achieve what we may have once thought was impossible.

Notes

What is my next move?

_____

_____

_____

_____

_____

_____

_____

_____

What specifically am I going to work on?

_____

_____

_____

_____

_____

_____

_____

_____

_____

Dr. Rudolph A. Moseley, Jr.

CHAPTER 2: BELIEF

Some people say I have an? attitude - maybe I do... but I think you have to. You have to believe in yourself when no one else does - that makes you a winner right there.

—Venus Williams

Be·lief (*noun*)

An acceptance that a statement is true or that something exists.

his belief in the value of hard work

trust, faith, or confidence in someone or something.

a belief in democratic politics

Belief in oneself is one of the most powerful factors that can determine whether or not you will be successful. Belief speaks of how we perceive ourselves. How we view ourselves has a tremendous impact on our ability to move forward when we are faced with difficulty. When I was in the eighth grade, I was not a model student. Unfortunately, I gave my teacher a hard time. And

11

she, maybe justifiably frustrated, made a statement that no child should ever hear. She looked at me and said in front of the class , "Rudy Moseley you are not going to amount to anything." At the time I played it off as though the words did not hurt me but these words negatively impacted how I viewed myself. They impacted how I viewed my ability to be successful in academic settings. Each time I turned in an assignment, if I did not get a successful grade, I would hear the words from this teacher.

Later in life, I realized that I had to choose what I was going to believe. Was I going to believe the statements made by that teacher or was I going to believe the positive statements spoken over my life by my parents? I was at a crossroads every time I was faced with a difficult academic obstacle. Would I let that teacher's words come true, or was I going to prove her wrong? As I was going to school, I could've allowed what that teacher said about me to overshadow and hinder how I viewed myself. But as time went on, and I continued with my academic career in college and university I began to discover who I was. I began to understand how powerful I was. I began to view myself as being a very smart person, The more I began to view myself as one who is gifted, talented, and brilliant, my area of expertise grew. This change in my perception of myself allowed me to persevere and accomplish many milestones, from becoming the youngest principal in the State of Rhode Island at age twenty-eight, to becoming an author, a speaker, a founding pastor, and an educator as well as several different feats that I did not think I would have been able to accomplish. I was able to do it because I believed in myself.

Never allow someone's opinion of you today to rob you of your future tomorrow. Young person, as you are reading this book, I want you to believe in yourself and believe that you are capable of doing more than what you've done thus far. I want you to believe that the sky's the limit. I want you to look at yourself in the mirror and I want to tell yourself that you are magnificent. You are powerful. You are valuable. You do have value, and I want you to see yourself as a person who is going to make a valuable contribution to the Earth.

I can remember being in English class during my freshman year of college. This class was heavy in both reading and writing, the two areas that I struggled with immensely. I remembered getting back my first assignment and not being able to understand what I did wrong because of all of the red marks. I felt at that moment that my eight-grade teacher's prophecy was going to come true. I began to panic. But I took a step back and said "let me try and get help because I could not do it on my own". I believed that I could do better but needed help on how to do it. I was not going to allow my one poor/failing to define my value or my worth. I got the help and did well in the class.

As I think about what is needed for success, I want you to believe in yourself. I want you to block all the naysayers. I want you to block all of the negativity. I want you to block all the haters. I want you to look in the mirror and I want you to see yourself as a champion to see yourself as victorious to see yourself as successful. When you approach your next academic challenge, I want you to look at it and say "I can do this, I can achieve great things. I can perform at a high-level." You were born for this you would not have come to this point in your life if it were not meant for you to be successful at this particular assignment. You were born to be a solution to a problem and to be the answer to somebody's dilemma. I want you to believe in yourself knowing that you have something to contribute. You have something to deposit, something to leave on this Earth that is valuable. I want you to believe in yourself today.

Notes

What is my next move?

_____

_____

_____

_____

_____

_____

_____

What specifically am I going to work on?

_____

_____

_____

_____

_____

_____

_____

_____

_____

Dr. Rudolph A. Moseley, Jr.

CHAPTER 3: CONFIDENCE

A man cannot be comfortable without his own approval.

—Mark Twain

Con·fi·dence (*noun*)

the feeling or belief that one can rely on someone or something; firm trust.

We had every confidence in the staff to handle the crisis.

During my sophomore year of college, I took anatomy and physiology. Passing this course was crucial because I was a biology major and chemistry minor. These courses were not easy and required focused attention. I was unsuccessful the first time I took this class because I underestimated the level of focus and dedication required to excel in a course at this level. STEM (Science Technology English and Math) courses are not easy. They are not impossible but do require undivided attention. At the start of the following semester, I had to retake the course as it was part of my major. When I took the course the second time I applied myself better than I did the first time and studied a little harder. For the first test, I not only engaged more with the material but I also spent more time with both my tutor and with the teaching assistant. When the first test results came back, I was successful. When I took the test I was confident that I was going to do better the second because I was prepared. My lack of success in the previous attempt was not because of a lack in my academic ability but in my time management and approach to the course. Your confidence will always be better when you have prepared better. Once you have prepared yourself, there is nothing that you can't accomplish. Confidence is necessary especially after experiencing failure.

Bill Gates who is widely known as one of the wealthiest people in the world, failed miserably at his first business. The name of his first company was Traf-O-Data (a device which could read traffic tapes and process the data). The company failed because the product failed. This did not stop Gates and his partner. In fact, it is well documented that this failure provided the foundation for their next product: Microsoft. Gates had to have confidence after failure. He had to be willing to try again. And, as we all know now, his contribution has changed the course of history.

I have confidence in your ability to make a difference. I have confidence in the fact that you will make a lasting contribution in the Earth and a positive change in the world. Every person is born with a gift, talent, and ability. Every person was born with an assignment. With that belief in mind, I have confidence that once you discover who you are, and why you're here, you will do great things in this world.

Mark Twain wrote that the two most important days in your life are the day you were born and the day you find out why. Finding out why you are here, will fuel your confidence to go forward and do some great things.

Notes

What is my next move?

_____

_____

_____

_____

_____

_____

_____

_____

What specifically am I going to work on?

_____

_____

_____

_____

_____

_____

_____

_____

_____

CHAPTER 4: DETERMINATION

The world's greatest achievers have been those who have always stayed focused on their goals and have been consistent in their efforts.

—Dr. Roopleen

De·ter·mi·na·tion *(noun)*

Firmness of purpose; resoluteness.

Determination is all about drawing a line in the sand and saying "I refuse to quit and I refuse to give up." The difference between successful people and unsuccessful people is that successful people continue to try even though they don't feel like it. Success oftentimes is right around the corner but sometimes we don't persist and we don't push through to get to that breakthrough. To be a winner and to be successful in your academics and to reach your full potential, you have to decide by saying to yourself "I am going to succeed. I am going to make my family proud. I am going to live up to my family name and make it great. I am determined not to be a failure. Even though I might not be successful at this class I am going to do whatever it takes because this is not going to beat me. Ultimately I am going to win.

As a track and field athlete at the University of Nebraska-Lincoln, I would occasionally get shin splints because of the pounding on my legs as a long jump and triple jumper. There were many times during practices when I was in severe pain. But I pushed through the pain because I wanted to improve, and I can remember my sophomore year improving to a personal best of 22 ' 5" in the long jump, and helping my team win that track meet. I felt extremely proud because I beat my personal best from the previous year. I paid a price to be successful. I paid a price to reach my goal. I paid a price to win. Many successful people have written songs or have had inventions or given public speeches that failed. A letdown does not mean that you are a failure. It is simply an opportunity for you to learn what you need to improve so you could be successful the next time. Only those who are determined to improve will succeed. Determination is developing the will to win.

What I want you to think about right now is the fact that you are determined to be successful at whichever level in life you find yourself. Even though you may have been unsuccessful at times, it doesn't mean that you are a failure. One setback does not define you; it is now how you finish the race that is important, finishing the race is what matters.. As a student, you have to be determined that you are going to be successful. Get that resolved down on the inside. Determine deep within yourself you are going to win.

Notes

What is my next move?

_____

_____

_____

_____

_____

_____

_____

What specifically am I going to work on?

_____

_____

_____

_____

_____

_____

_____

_____

Chapter 5: Excellence

Excellence is never an accident. It is always the result of high intention, sincere effort, and intelligent execution; it represents the wise choice of many alternatives - choice, not chance, determines your destiny.

—Aristotle

Ex·cel·lence *(noun)*

the quality of being outstanding or extremely good

Related word: ex·cel (verb) be exceptionally good at or proficient in an activity or subject.

There have been times in my life when I knew I could do better, but I settled for just enough. I knew I could have gotten a higher score. I knew I could have tried harder in that last run, on that paper, or that project. I just did not have a standard of excellence. I did not want to outshine others. I did not want to be excellent because that was not celebrated by my peers. So, I had a couple of things going on. On the one hand, I had to overcome laziness and procrastination. On the other hand, there were times I had to be comfortable with doing well.

The quality of being excellent is one that is in the reach of every individual. Many of us settle for average. Many of us settle for just enough. But to be a star, to be successful, you must be intentional about being excellent. You have to make a decision. It is talking to yourself and telling your inner self that excellence is going to be your habit. I am going to push myself to be excellent.

Excellence is the quality of being outstanding, the quality of being set apart. It is said that excellence is not an accident. Excellence comes about when we are extremely intentional.

In my house growing up, excellence was the expected standard. My mother would say, "do your best and forget the rest." She insisted that my best was the only thing that was ever good enough.

Once in seventh grade, I came home, and handed my father my report card. In those days each student was ranked based on their average in all of the subjects. That first semester I was ranked twenty-eight out of a possible thirty-two students. That was fourth from the bottom. There was a time where I did not do my best and my parents demanded better results from me. "What is this, what is this? My father demanded to know when he opened the report. "This is not you. this is not a reflection of your work; this is not a reflection of your best work." At that moment I was terrified because he did not ask the questions in the most understanding tone. He both challenged me and warned me. He said if I did not put forth my best effort for this final semester there would be a serious consequence waiting for me at the end of the term. My butt could only imagine the kind of consequences he was talking about. That stern warning was all that I needed to bring out my best work. Would you believe that for the very next semester I came first in class in mathematics with an overall rank of seventh in the class? I learned during that season that I had more to offer. Before, I was clearly not bringing my best game. I was holding back. I was not living up to my full potential. I had to put aside the foolishness and focus on being the best me that I could. And to my surprise, the best me was quite good. What it also showed me was by putting forth my effort to be the best revealed that I was the best.

There are many of us who, if we tried just a little bit harder would also discover that there is greatness on the inside. I dare you to set a standard of excellence and see how good you could be, how high could you possibly go, and how excellent your work could become. I want to challenge you today to have a spirit of excellence in everything that you do. Mediocrity is never good enough. My mother's words still ring in my heart today. Her insistence on excellence has taught me the value of hard work and has helped me to reap its benefits.

Notes

What is my next move?

_____

_____

_____

_____

_____

_____

_____

_____

What specifically am I going to work on?

_____

_____

_____

_____

_____

_____

_____

_____

_____

_____

Dr. Rudolph A. Moseley, Jr.

CHAPTER 6: FAITH

Faith is not belief without proof, but trust without reservation.

—*D. Elton Trueblood*

Faith *(noun)*

complete trust or confidence in someone or something.

Do you believe in the dreams you have? Do you believe that your future is bright? Faith and success are inseparable. Faith is like the person you met that is the perfect match for you. You don't ever want to be out of their presence. You just enjoy their company because of what they produce in you. Faith is like the friend you enjoy doing life with. You know, your friend that you enjoy doing projects with because you two work so well together. Faith, according to the definition, is having confidence in someone or something. And, that someone is you. Faith is your companion on the journey to making your dreams a reality.

To be successful you have to have faith in yourself. You have to believe that if you put forth the effort, the time, and the energy, you will reap what you have sown. If you make it a habit to be your best, to be excellent, and to have the attitude of a winner, you will always be on top and never at the bottom. You must be a person who trusts the process. This is the success formula. Success does not automatically happen. Success happens as a result of intentional steps taken in faith. To believe in yourself despite past failures is fundamental. You must have faith that as you do some things differently you will get different outcomes especially if you have just experienced failure. Faith is the belief that what I can't see is possible. Faith is the belief in the fact that though an obstacle may be big, I can overcome, so I keep moving forward. Faith is the belief that even though I might be a struggling reader, that if I continue to read, I will get better. Faith is the belief that even though I might struggle in math, if I continue to practice, I will improve. Faith says I believe that even though a teacher may have said something negative about me, I am going to succeed. I'm not going to allow the opinions of others to stop me from what I know I can achieve. Faith says that nothing is impossible. Faith says that I can make it.

Growing up, I struggled with reading. This learning difference had an incredible impact on my educational career. When I took the SATs, I did horribly on the English section of the exam. If I had allowed the results of that test to define my future, I would not be where I am today. I can now look at my past report cards, at some of the courses I struggled with in middle and high school, and based on those results I know I have defied the odds. I had faith that I had something to say. I had faith that I had something to contribute. I had faith to know that I have something on the inside that needs to get out - an insatiable desire to help others be the best they can be. I had to have faith in myself and the confidence that I could make a difference in the world. You must commit and press forward.

You too must believe and have faith, so that you can achieve. You must believe that your past does not define you, and past mistakes don't have to define your tomorrow. You have to have faith that you are valuable, that you are unique and that you have a valuable gift. You have something to contribute to the world. You have to have faith that there's some greatness on the inside of you that needs to come out and needs to be shared with the rest of the world. Your existence is proof that there is something for you to do. Your life is necessary. You have to have faith in God and believe that with God in all things are possible.

I want to encourage you today to have faith in the process and to have faith in yourself. I want you to know that all of your hard work is going to pay off.

Notes

What is my next move?

_____

_____

_____

_____

_____

_____

_____

_____

What specifically am I going to work on?

_____

_____

_____

_____

_____

_____

_____

_____

_____

_____

Dr. Rudolph A. Moseley, Jr.

CHAPTER 7: GOALS

The mystery of human existence lies not in just staying alive, but in finding something to live for. —Fyodor Dostoyevsky, The Brothers Karamazov

Goal (*noun*)

the result or achievement toward which effort is directed; aim; end.

The team worked together to reach their goal.

Life is all about goals. The goals we set are the goals we get. Goals represent something that you're shooting for, something that you're striving for, and something that determines how and where you spend your time. Everyone has people that they admire and look up to. When we think about our own lives we think about what we would like to achieve. We also think about how we would like to be remembered. These are the popular goals. When we think about our Instagram, Facebook, or Twitter or the next social media platforms and we think about how many likes we get, we have a goal of being liked by people, and the goal of being admired or followed by people. We project a certain image, and do certain things on these platforms so that we can achieve that goal. When it comes to academic achievement and academic effort, we have to do the same thing, set goals.

Likewise, we also have to set the goal to be the best student that we're going to be. When we set goals like this, to achieve high academic standards, we may not hit that mark all the time. When this happens we have to adjust the goal or we may have to reevaluate our goals or we may have to reevaluate our strategy. No matter what, we must have something that we're shooting for. If we don't have something that we're shooting for, then any other idea can create a distraction and take us off course to a place that we did not want to go.

At the beginning of the school year, I would often ask students who has a goal of getting an A in their classes for the year. Then I would ask the question at the end of the term and at the end of the year who achieved their goal. Some students achieved their goal, some came close, and some did not. I asked the students that did not meet their goal what happened. They often said, "I could have met my goals but was unwilling to put in the work." It had nothing to do with ability but everything to do with effort.

In life, goals we set are the goals we get, when we work towards those goals. Hard work pays off. Nothing in life happens without hard work commitment and dedication.

We celebrate people who accomplish great things. The reason why we celebrate them is that they made pulled off a great achievement. To accomplish that, they had to set a goal. Next, they had to map out a plan. Then they had to follow the plan to achieve that goal. So if you're in school right now and you have a goal to make the Dean's List, you first have to find out what it is going to take to meet the requirements to make the Dean's List. Academic achievement is no different than athletic achievement. You set the goal, and then you work towards that goal. I want to encourage you to set and then to press.

In my life I've set goals. I've set financial goals. I've set educational goals. I've even set a goal for the kind of father that I want to be to my children, and some of those goals guided me through my life. The goals I have set have impacted my life choices. They impacted what types of relationships I got into and what potential relationships I ran away from.

I have a goal for the type of legacy that I want to leave. I have a goal for the kind of name I want to have on the Earth. I hope that as you read this book you'll allow your dreams to take you to the place of your potential. I hope that you set a high bar for yourself, and never settle for average. I hope that you will allow high standards to guide your life and guide your values. I hope that you will live this way so that you leave a contribution on this earth that will never be forgotten.

I hope that as you read this book that you won't wait until you're old to set goals. Set goals now. Set goals early so that you can be all you were intended to be. I finished high school at sixteen years old. I finished college with my first degree at 20. I became the youngest principal in the state of Rhode Island at twenty-eight years old, and I continue to make a difference in the lives of youth.

Goals are powerful because they fuel your why. Your why is what fuels your reasons. Your reasons for doing things are extremely powerful in your mind because they drive you when you want to quit. Goals are essential for success because they give you something to shoot for. Everything begins with a vision, and visions are then broken down into goals. Goals are the benchmarks that we shoot for to make our vision become a reality. Goals are the building blocks to success. Goals are the foundation upon which structure is built. Young person, if you don't shoot for something, then you will be blown into anything.

Notes

What is my next move?

_____

_____

_____

_____

_____

_____

_____

_____

What specifically am I going to work on?

_____

_____

_____

_____

_____

_____

_____

_____

Dr. Rudolph A. Moseley, Jr.

Chapter 8: Hard work

The price of success is hard work, dedication to the job at hand, and the determination that whether we win or lose, we have applied the best of ourselves to the task at hand.

—*Vince Lombardi*

Hard work (*noun*)

a great deal of effort or endurance.

The price of success is hard work, dedication to the job at hand, and the determination that whether we win or lose, we have applied the best of ourselves to the task at hand.

It is impossible to be successful in anything meaningful without hard work. Hard work speaks to the commitment to the grind. It speaks of focus, determination, direction, and the discipline to put off the pleasure of the present for the success of the future. Hard Work speaks of doing now what others will not do today to have in the future what others are not able to attain.

In high school I wanted to make the junior national team for track and field. There was a certain level of dedication that was required to be good enough to be selected. I had the potential to make the team but hard work was necessary to pull out the potential that was already stored.

None of the achievements that I have made in my life thus far came easy. To achieve the level of success I have, whether it was my high school diploma or my bachelor's degree or my master's degree or my doctoral degree, it required a level of focused determination and dedication. In order for me to become an Academic All-American in college, there was a level of hard work that was required to reach that particular achievement. Hard work is necessary both on and off the field. Hard work is necessary on the field no matter what your sport is, and hard work is necessary in the classroom no matter what your field of study. Anybody who is successful in life will tell you that they did not achieve their success without hard work.

I want to encourage you not to be afraid of hard work because hard work always pays off. Just because something is hard doesn't mean that it's impossible. Oftentimes in school we get discouraged from going after a goal because it didn't come easily. But nothing worth anything comes easy. Everything that is worth something has to be fought for. Once the price has been paid, then you can tell the true value. The truth of the matter is that if it were easy everyone would be doing it.

The fact that you made a decision to focus in this particular direction you will receive the rewards of that focused attention. I think back to my college years when I was taking microbiology. It was another class that was necessary for my degree. I had an upcoming exam, and I stayed up until 2 o'clock in the morning studying. Did I want to go to the party? Yes. Did I want to hang out with friends? Yes. Did I want to sleep? Yes. But the desire to succeed was greater than the pull of anything else. I felt extremely satisfied and honored after passing the exam and receiving my degree in biology, becoming or making me one of the first African American males to receive a degree in biology from the University of Nebraska in the past decade. And, I also happened to be an athlete. I was honored to have received that degree. Was it hard? Absolutely! Was it worth it? You better believe it!

As you focus on becoming successful in your life I want you to consider the price that needs to be paid. I don't want you to give up just because it's difficult or just because it's hard, or just because it might be confusing. I want you to understand that this is the culture of success. The culture of success is one of commitment, sacrifice, dedication, persistence and follow-through. I want you to learn this lesson early so that you can be successful in whatever it is that you're going to put your mind and heart to in the future.

Notes

What is my next move?

_____

_____

_____

_____

_____

_____

_____

_____

What specifically am I going to work on?

_____

_____

_____

_____

_____

_____

_____

_____

Dr. Rudolph A. Moseley, Jr.

CHAPTER 9: IDEAS

The mind, once stretched by a new idea, never returns to its original dimensions.

—Ralph Waldo Emerson

I·de·a (*noun*)

a thought or suggestion as to a possible course of action.

The mind, once stretched by a new idea, never returns to its original dimensions.

Ideas are the most powerful things on the face of this earth. Everything you see, hear, feel, touch, and taste all began with an idea. Every solution, every breakthrough, every invention, all began with an idea. The greatest problem to hit our modern world has been COVID-19 and the Corona Virus. Life as we once knew had been interrupted. Scientists have been working feverishly to develop a cure. In the meantime, they have had some ideas that have been rolled out in various societies to help save lives. Ideas regarding a cure have been talked about, shared and discussed and tested until a solution is found. Ideas are powerful. They shape life as we know it.

Ideas begin in the place called the imagination. The imagination is the place where plans originate. The ideas first begin as pictures, images, thoughts. It is the place in your mind where your ideas reside. I call it "image nation" because it is the residence for your ideas. Ideas are powerful because they affect beliefs. Ideas affect even our self-perception, how we view ourselves, whether it is good or bad. These perceptions all have their origination in your ideas. I want to encourage you as a young person to say to yourself "I have good ideas." You have good ideas because you were created to solve a problem. You were created as a solution to a dilemma. You have the answer that many people are searching for. Your existence is a testament to the fact that you were created to solve the problem. This means that you are carrying a solution. The solution has its genesis in your mind. Your life is necessary. Your life has value.

As a young student in elementary school whenever the teacher asked a question, I would hesitate to raise my hand to give a solution or an answer to the problem because I didn't think that my ideas were good enough to share with the classroom. To my amazement, after some time of waiting, I would hear somebody else give the same solution that I was thinking about. I want you to have the courage to share your ideas and not miss out on opportunities because of the fear of failure. Just because your idea may not be the best solution, don't keep it to yourself. Sharing ideas helps you with the thinking process to understand that you do have something to contribute, and something to offer. When you share your ideas you discover also that your idea may add to someone else's idea.

I struggled through high school and throughout college with the fear of sharing my ideas in a public forum. I was hesitant because as I listened to some of the responses to questions they were different from my own. Because I didn't think I was good enough,I would not share what was going on in my own mind. It wasn't until I got older and got confident about the fact that my unique gifting and unique creative ability was what made me special that I started sharing my ideas. I now embrace the fact that I think differently. There are times when I would look at something from a very different perspective. I now know that this is what makes me valuable, a realization that I have grown to accept.

I want to encourage you to practice sharing your thinking in public space. I want you to practice letting people know what is really going on in your mind. I don't want you to ever feel as though you're not smart or that you're stupid because you see things differently. Ideas can and should be expanded. You must be a reader. I want to encourage you to read. I want to encourage you to be respectful of other people's ideas. Reading is an engagement with somebody else's thoughts. When you read a book you're reading someone's thoughts put to paper. As you read books, you have a chance to have dialogues with the author. As you read their ideas they will expand your own.

I want to encourage you to share your ideas. I also want to encourage you to study and read about your ideas so that they can become even larger. As you read and study and listen to others, you then become even more of an expert in regards to what you're thinking. No longer will you be someone that people overlook or pass over. You'll be a person that people look to. Because you shared your thinking with the larger community, people will be encouraged by you. You will be celebrated for your great ideas on a curtain topic, and will be respected as a thought leader in your field.

Notes

What is my next move?

_____

_____

_____

_____

_____

_____

_____

_____

What specifically am I going to work on?

_____

_____

_____

_____

_____

_____

_____

_____

_____

Dr. Rudolph A. Moseley, Jr.

CHAPTER 10: JOSTLE

No man lives without jostling and being jostled; in all ways he has to elbow himself through the world, giving and receiving offense

—Thomas Carlyle

Jos·tle (*verb*)

push, elbow, or bump against (someone) roughly, typically in a crowd.

Today I choose life. Every morning when I wake up I can choose joy, happiness, negativity, pain... To feel the freedom that comes from being able to continue to make mistakes and choices - today I choose to feel life, not to deny my humanity but embrace it.

There are times in life when you have to fight – fight for what you believe in, fight for what is right and true, fight for your dream and your destiny. Anything in life worth anything does not come easy. To have something worthwhile is usually an uphill battle. At times you not only have to fight against the haters but sometimes you have to fight against your own self-talk. You have to fight against your own self-negativity.

As the definition states, to jostle means to the elbow, to push, and to bump against. There are times where you have to fight away things that were said about you that were not true. It takes discipline of thought which is the discipline in your mind to wrestle those negative thoughts down. It is the process where you do not allow these negative thoughts to park or take residence in your mind. It takes a focused effort to replace negative statements with positive statements.

There are times when you have to fight - fight for what you believe in, fight for what is right and what is true. Fight for your dream and for your destiny. You have to fight for your future.

You must remind yourself repeatedly about what you're fighting for. I think about the time in my life when I had to fight for my degrees. The completion of those degrees was not easy. There were times when I was tired and discouraged and had to fight against thoughts of "you don't belong here," "you're not smart enough," or "You're not good enough." I had to fight against the question of "Do you have the stamina to complete the road that you embark upon?"

In life, we all have to make choices and we have to make decisions about who exactly we want to become. Life is a choice. It's all about what you make of it. It's all about what you make out of it. You get out of life what you put in. In life, you reap what you sow. The person that you're staring at in the mirror may not be the person that you like or the person that you have in your mind. To jostle means you have to fight for what you believe in and fight for what is valuable to you. You owe it to yourself to fight for the best version of yourself. You owe it to yourself to fight for the future that you envision. You owe it to yourself to add to the world and to give your life away. You owe to the world to be the best version of yourself that commit to giving your best self away. I'm reminded of the verse from my favorite book, The Bible, that says that nobody fights not to win. Nobody starts the race not to win the prize. Everyone wants to be successful. Everybody wants to win. But there is a price that has to be paid. The price is the willingness to fight for what you believe in and to fight for what's important to you. You want to fight to become who you were destined to be.

You have so much potential. But that potential cannot be released unless there is a fight raging on the inside. I can remember as an athlete in my track days when I wanted to improve to get a personal best in the long jump. I remember that fight against the old pain in my shins from shin splints from pounding the hard ground for hours, day in and day out. My muscles were fatigued from doing squats and lifting hundreds of pounds. I had been really exhausted at times but I was willing to fight past my desire to quit because the goal of beating my personal best and the goal of improving was more important to me. I was willing to ignore the pain so that I could be successful. I want to encourage you to think about the obstacles that you have to fight against, the things that you have to push past. What are the things that are holding you back? Identify them so you know exactly what your opponent is. When you study your opponent that's when you can defeat your opponent even if the opponent is self-talk in your own mind. We fight to win. We play the game to win. Victory is flowing through our veins.

If you know the enemy and know yourself, you need not fear the result of a hundred battles. If you know yourself but not the enemy, for every victory gained you will also suffer a defeat. If you know neither the enemy nor yourself, you will succumb in every battle.

— Sun Tzu, The Art of War

Notes

What is my next move?

_____

_____

_____

_____

_____

_____

_____

_____

What specifically am I going to work on?

_____

_____

_____

_____

_____

_____

_____

_____

Dr. Rudolph A. Moseley, Jr.

CHAPTER 11: KNOWLEDGE

To know what you know and what you do not know is knowledge.

—Confucius

Knowl·edge *(noun)*

Facts, information, and skills acquired by a person through experience or education; the theoretical or practical understanding of a subject.

Since the beginning of time people have been hungry for knowledge. This insatiable thirst has been the motivation that has led to all of the discoveries in the earth. This curiosity has been the catalyst to the revelation of many breakthroughs. To be successful you have to be a person that is thirsty for knowledge. A common mistake that many students make is that they think that when they know something about a topic that means that they know everything about that topic. You have to be a person that is thirsty for the right information and be a person who is hungry and thirsty for more information. This new information helps you to be skilled at what you do.

I can remember that when I was young I didn't like to read. The reason why I didn't like to read was because I struggled with making sense of the words. I also struggled with comprehending what the sentences meant. As a result, I avoided reading. It wasn't until I got to college that I found out what I was passionate about in terms of education. Once I discovered my passion, reading became purposeful. This purpose was enough for me to push through the difficulty and push past the uncomfortableness and push past the uneasiness. As a result, I got better at reading. I recognized also that in order for me to go to the next level I needed to read. I needed to engage with the text and pull out the information so that I could be better at what I was gifted and called to do.

You can acquire knowledge in many different ways. Sometimes it may be in the form of a podcast, YouTube, CD or DVD. But most of the time books are the medium through which ideas are transferred. Ideas are what help us to make decisions about our next steps in life.

Leaders are readers and ideas rule the world. Knowledge is power. In ancient civilizations when the captor wanted to keep the captive bound and powerless they did it by keeping knowledge from them. My hope is that as you pursue your purpose and you pursue your passion that you will understand that you become better when you focus on getting knowledge because people perish for a lack of knowledge.

Notes

What is my next move?

_____

_____

_____

_____

_____

_____

_____

What specifically am I going to work on?

_____

_____

_____

_____

_____

_____

_____

_____

CHAPTER 12

LOVE FOR LEARNING

Education is the passport to the future, for tomorrow belongs to those who prepare for it today.

—Malcolm X

Learn·ing (*noun*)

the acquisition of knowledge or skills through experience, study, or by being taught.

These children experienced difficulties in learning.

Much like the thirst for knowledge, the love for learning, the hunger for information, and the drive to pursue are factors necessary to activate the potential on the inside of every person.

A love for learning is a necessity in order for anyone to be successful in the calling that they have been gifted to complete. A love for learning is the desire to acquire more information, education, and skills to improve upon your gift. Everyone has a gift. Everyone came with a gift. Those who are diligent in their gift won't serve before ordinary people. In fact, they will be celebrated and honored because of their gift. Their value would be appreciated by many. There are many people who desire to be successful. There are many people who desire to be at the top of their game. However, few are willing to pay the price of success. To be successful you have to be diligent and disciplined. This diligence and discipline is characterized by having the love for learning to acquire the knowledge and the skills necessary to maximize the treasure that is on the inside of you.

There are many who do not like to read but remember, as I said before, leaders are readers. I would say that there aren't many people who like to read. The question is, "what type of material are you reading? "Because when you take time to study yourself and discover your unique value, you are then in a position to know exactly what type of material you should be spending time with. You will know the material that will fuel you. You will know the material that will excite you and expand you. You will discover the material that will stretch you. Before you decide on what type of material to read, you must first study yourself to know the purpose of the new information. This information and revelation also fuel what you major in when you get to college and determine what type of workshops and seminars you sign up for, and which YouTube videos you watch.

I struggled with the discipline to read until I discovered my unique value. I love personal growth, development, and leadership. I also love to help people. So I love to study so that I can improve the level of service I provide as I help people better and at a high level. What fuels your passion is an indicator of your gifting and also your assignment. What gets you excited is another clue to where you should be spending your time. You have strengths and you should work to strengthen your strengths even more. Even after having one of the highest degrees you can ever get, I still love learning. I specifically love learning about what I am called to do. This will help you as you continue to grow through life.

Notes

What is my next move?

_____

_____

_____

_____

_____

_____

_____

_____

What specifically am I going to work on?

_____

_____

_____

_____

_____

_____

_____

_____

_____

CHAPTER 13

MAKE A DIFFERENCE

The world is waiting for you, never give up on your dream(s). Arise and make an impact, there are people who are just waiting for your story which will give them a turnaround in their lives. It can be the message of the gospel, motivation, inspiration, etc. You need to spread that message; you CAN'T KEEP it to yourself. I dare you to Make a Difference. —Wisdom Kwashie Mensah

---

Make a difference (verb)

1 the state or quality of being unlike

2 a specific instance of being unlike

3 a distinguishing mark or feature

There was a story that I read about a little girl who was walking on the beach after a storm. The storm was very violent and the tide was pretty high. Unfortunately, hundreds of starfish were stranded on the shore. The little girl decided that she could make a difference. So she started at the beginning of the beach and began throwing the starfish back into the ocean one starfish at a time. She continued for hours. A man was watching as she diligently and carefully picked up each starfish and proceeded to throw it back into the ocean. The man was so curious because in spite of all of her time and effort there were still hundreds of starfish left. He got off his chair and walked down to the beach to ask her why she was doing this. When he got to her, he told her that there were too many to help, and asked if she thought she was making a difference. She told the man that it may not look like she is making a difference but she did make a difference in the life of every starfish that she picked up and returned to the ocean. In spite of what it looked like and in the face of a very difficult situation she decided that she was going to make a difference.

You have the ability to make a difference and make an impact. One thing that all successful people have in common is that they have taken the road less traveled. What does that mean? It means that they recognize their unique difference. They worked on improving that skill. They honed their uniqueness and then presented that uniqueness to solve a problem. We are all problem solvers. We are all innovators. We are all world changers. We were all sent here on an assignment to make a difference in the world. Your uniqueness is your value. The characteristics that set you apart is actually what makes you most valuable. Your contribution to the world is what makes for a significant life. At your young age you may not be sure what exactly that contribution is but finding this out is your primary responsibility. Author Mark Twain said it best, that the two most important days in your life are the day you were born and the day you find out why. Live your life on purpose. Live to be a history maker. Live to leave your mark that could never be erased.

I can remember my mother asked what I wanted to be when I grew up. I told her that I wanted to stand on the side of the road and give cans to people and help those in need. Looking back I can see that I had an idea of what I wanted to do with my life at a young age, helping people. Helping people is what causes you to make a difference. Serving people is what actually makes you great. Living to serve is the motivating factor. Instead of asking what can I do to make money? Ask yourself. "How many people can I serve today?, what can I do to serve. How can I help you today. How can I be at my best to serve you in the best way possible?" Setting this standard for your life will set you up for success now and in the future. This is living at a very high level.

Notes

What is my next move?

_____

_____

_____

_____

_____

_____

_____

_____

What specifically am I going to work on?

_____

_____

_____

_____

_____

_____

_____

_____

CHAPTER 14 : NAVIGATION

True navigation begins in the human heart. It's the most important
map of all.

—*Elizabeth Kapu'uwailani Lindsey*

Nav·i·ga·tion *(noun)*

the process or activity of accurately ascertaining one's position and planning and following a route.

When I was in school a young man came up to me and asked me if I wanted to sell drugs. I told him no because that activity did not line up with my desire to become a doctor. At that time my goal was to become a doctor. I can also remember when I was in college and was approached by another young man who asked if I wanted to take drugs, and again my answer was no. The reason was that abusing drugs did not line up with my dream of being the best college athlete that I could be. Life is filled with choices. Knowing where you are headed will always help to say no to what does not help you towards your dream. The pull of the future will always help you to overcome the temporary setbacks and temptations in your present.

John Maxwell writes, "plan your life and then live your plan." Many successful people did not become successful by accident. They became successful through what is called intentional living. They had a dream, created a plan for that dream to become a reality and then they followed that plan. So no matter what stage you are in life it always starts with a vision. Where there is no vision, people give up and they lose hope. This vision also helps you to make decisions. It helps you to know what to say yes to and what to say no to.

To be successful you have to know where you want to go. I want you to know where you want to go. Then you're able to chart the course. This decision impacts how you are going to get there. Navigation is knowing where you want to be and then mapping it out. After the plan is laid out then we have to follow the plan. This begins with the belief in yourself that you can be successful. You must also believe that your life has value. It begins with the belief that your life has meaning. Once you have a vision in your heart for what contribution you're going to make you can then design a pathway and then you follow that plan. For example, you may have a plan to be a college graduate. This means that you would have to graduate from high school and then focus on your major course of study in college. You can do it. I know you can focus. Get a dream for your life then design a plan that will get you there. Then follow your plan.

Notes

What is my next move?

_____

_____

_____

_____

_____

_____

_____

_____

What specifically am I going to work on?

_____

_____

_____

_____

_____

_____

_____

_____

_____

Chapter 15: Obsession

When passion meets inspiration, an obsession is born.

—Anonymous

Ob·ses·sion *(noun)*

an idea or thought that continually preoccupies or intrudes on a person's mind.

Obsession is often looked at as a negative thing. However, obsession is necessary to bring focus. To be successful many people have to identify and discover what they are passionate about. People have to figure out what makes them excited, what their driving force is, what makes them tick, what makes them excited and what brings them joy. Obsession is powerful because it fuels inspiration. Inspiration gives birth to imagination and creativity that fuels the drive from the inside to make a difference, solve a problem or to create a solution. When you become passionate about something and passionate about its success and your future achievements, you begin to see and set goals. You develop an internal drive where nobody needs to police you anymore. You have learned how to police yourself. You need no external motivation because you have found your internal inspiration.

As a driver of yourself, you become the person that is the steward of your future. You understand in life you are responsible for the kind of life you are going to live. It is very critical that you identify what you are passionate about because what you're passionate about is key to your greatness. It's key to your uniqueness. It's the key to your power. Your passion and obsession will help you to be a good steward of your vision. I think about when I got the vision to write this book how I became obsessed with seeing it through to completion. I knew that the book was going to make a difference in the lives of people. I understood what I was focusing on in my life and how I became obsessed about achieving a goal. I saw the value in the achievement of this goal. I saw how this book was going to make a difference. I hope you become obsessed with getting good grades. I hope you become obsessed with being the best student that you could be. I hope you become obsessed with achieving your vision. I hope you become obsessed with being great and meeting your potential.

Notes

What is my next move?

_____

_____

_____

_____

_____

_____

_____

_____

What specifically am I going to work on?

_____

_____

_____

_____

_____

_____

_____

_____

_____

Dr. Rudolph A. Moseley, Jr.

CHAPTER 16: PASSION

Every great dream begins with a dreamer. Always remember, you have within you the strength, the patience, and the passion to reach for the stars to change the world.

—*Harriet Tubman*

Pas·sion *(noun)*

strong and barely controllable emotion.

a man of impetuous passion.

It was the middle of my sixth grade year when I began to notice a particularly pretty young girl by the name of Shelly. She was beautiful. I would tell my friend Desmond that I would love to tell her how I felt but was too afraid. I was afraid of being rejected. One day at recess Desmond suggested that I write her a note to tell her how I felt with the check box "yes" or "no" to find out if she felt the same. I was deathly afraid but nonetheless because of my passion for her I wrote the note and then gave it to her. She was shocked to receive the note and unfortunately, took it to the principal. As I look back my passion was so strong that I was willing to take a risk to achieve a goal.

Passion is an incredible emotion that is necessary for anything of significance to be accomplished. You cannot overcome mediocrity and being average without being passionate about something. When you become passionate about something you become driven. When you become passionate about something you become obsessed with it. You also become driven and your reasons push you to do things that you wouldn't normally do. Passion causes you to do things the average person would not do to get extraordinary results that others may never achieve. Every successful person started with being passionate about something. Passion causes you to become focused, and when you become focused, you become dangerous. You become dangerous because you are now single in your focus.

People who are passionate focus all of their energy and talents in pursuit of their vision. They focus on the one thing that you were called and created to address. Passion is an awesome feeling. Passion is an awesome emotion and is something that is God-given so that you can achieve greatness. Passion is what causes you to get up when you've been knocked down. Passion causes you to rise up when others want to bring you down. Passion is what causes you to try again when you failed the first time. Passion is what causes you to overcome in the face of difficulty. Passion is what makes you get up and try again. I'm passionate about education. I am passionate about making a difference. I am passionate about being an inspiration to others. Even when people have called me names because of my passion, it did not stop me. My passion to make a difference is what pushes me to continue to move forward.

Notes

What is my next move?

_____

_____

_____

_____

_____

_____

_____

_____

What specifically am I going to work on?

_____

_____

_____

_____

_____

_____

_____

_____

_____

Chapter 17: Quality People

Associate with men of good quality if you esteem your own reputation;
for it is better to be alone than in bad company.

—George Washington

Qual·i·ty *(noun)*

the standard of something as measured against other things of a similar kind; the degree of excellence of something.

When I was growing up my mother would always say "birds of a feather flock together." Understand that if you want to be successful you have to hang around with successful people. The Bible says that bad company corrupts good morals. You can't be around the pigpen and not come out smelling like pigs. So when you think about your life you must think about the direction that you want to go to. You have to ask yourself the question,"Are the people that I'm surrounded with going in the same direction that I am going in?" The Bible also speaks of the fact that it is impossible for two to walk together unless they agree.

Some people can have an agreement in terms of mission and vision but when it comes to values that's where the disagreement is going to come out. There are certain things that I value and certain things are important to me. These things make up my character. My character traits determine what values. When I am with somebody, my values influence my decisions and ultimately the direction in which I'm going to go. I only associate with people who are of good reputation, good quality, and people of integrity. As a result, we won't run the risk of having a disagreement because they may not see something as that bad but it's really bad to me because of my values. Only associate with quality people. If you want to be an eagle, you have to surround yourself with other eagles. If you want to be at the top of your game, you have to associate with people that are going in that direction.

There are many people who want what others have but are not willing to do what others did to get what they have. So many people talk about wanting to be successful. If you want to be successful, then begin to hang around successful people. You will begin to discover and understand their habits, actions and process. You can then imitate or incorporate these life hacks into your own life so that you can now become what you envision your life to be.

The world is based on the law; you reap whatever you sow. Everyone has the same twenty-four hours in the day, and everyone is breathing the same oxygen. The difference between the high-flyers and the low-flyers is information. They also put that information into practice. These people are not smarter or any more talented than you. The difference is that they have made a decision to live their life a certain way.

When I decided that I wanted to live a certain way, people began to exit my life. Was it painful to see them exit, yes? But it was necessary for me to get to the next level. I had a friend in college who was involved in some questionable activities. When I made the decision to focus on my studies and to not be associated with some of the illegal activities they were involved in, we separated as friends. Three days later one of the guys that I used to hang out with was charged with attempted murder. I did not know if I would have been in the car with them that night because I so wanted to be cool. But thank God my life and reputation was spared because I made the choice to let some people leave my life.

Notes

What is my next move?

_____

_____

_____

_____

_____

_____

_____

_____

What specifically am I going to work on?

_____

_____

_____

_____

_____

_____

_____

_____

CHAPTER 18: RESILIENT

Hold yourself responsible for a higher standard than anybody else expects of you. Never excuse yourself. Never pity yourself. Be a hard master to yourself-and be lenient to everybody else.

—*Henry Ward Beecher*

Re·sil·ient *(adjective)*

(of a person or animal) able to withstand or recover quickly from difficult conditions.

Life is very unpredictable no matter how hard you try, and no matter how good your plan, the reality is that you can't control everything. In life, the secret to being successful is how you respond when life hits you with a curve ball. Many people get excited about a dream and enthusiastic about a vision. They get excited and strategic about setting goals. We get so excited that we run to tell everyone. Then the separation happens between those who plan and those who execute. Very rarely are people willing to endure what is necessary to make that dream a reality.

The idea of resilience is one where I take a beating and keep on moving forward. I may have gotten knocked down but I am not out. Resilience speaks of consistency. I am consistent no matter what happens. I don't move, I'm not swayed and I'm not deterred. I might be distracted or delayed for a period of time but I get right back into where I need to be. Something may not have turned out the way I thought it would turn out but it doesn't mean that life is over. Resilience says I'm going to get up. I'm going to focus and I'm going to make lemonade when life deals me lemons.

In the summer of my freshman year, I registered for a course in physics. I was taking the course because I wanted to get ahead. One night I received a phone call and on the other end was my mother crying. She had called me to tell me that my grandfather was in a horrible car accident. She informed me that he had to be rushed to surgery but the doctors were on strike so he would not get medical care right away. My grandfather lived in rural Jamaica. I fell to my knees outside of the class and began to cry. My grandfather, Pops, was my world. Every summer for the past five years I spent time in Jamaica with Pops. A couple days passed, and I received the call that Pops did not make it. I did not want to continue going to class. I did not want to continue studying. I did not want to continue doing anything. I then thought about what my grandfather wanted from me. He was so proud that I was the first boy in my family to go to college, and he always told me that he believed in me. This realization made me press past what I was feeling. I pushed past the pain. I reminded myself that Pops would have wanted me to succeed for him. I went home for the funeral and came back and completed the summer course. I had to be resilient in the face of adversity, and I know you can do this as well. I said a long time ago that I was going to become a doctor. I did not become a medical doctor but a doctor of education. We all have goals, dreams, and aspirations. My hope is that you develop resilience to make your dream a reality.

Notes

What is my next move?

_____

_____

_____

_____

_____

_____

_____

_____

What specifically am I going to work on?

_____

_____

_____

_____

_____

_____

_____

_____

_____

Chapter 19: Self-Discipline

We do today what they won't, so tomorrow we can accomplish what they can't.

—Dwayne 'The Rock' Johnson

Self-dis·ci·pline (*noun*)

the ability to control one's feelings and overcome one's weaknesses; the ability to pursue what one thinks is right despite temptations to abandon it.

Self-discipline is the key to success. Self-discipline is policing yourself, to do what others are not willing to do today to have what others may never get tomorrow. Self-discipline is making the decisions necessary today so that tomorrow will take care of itself. You don't have to focus on the vision but the real struggle is the daily decisions that are necessary to accomplish the vision for tomorrow. Life is made up of a series of decisions. Where I am today is the product of my best thinking. These were all my decisions. I made a pledge to myself never to blame anyone for where I am in life. Life begins by taking responsibility for your current state. I cannot blame anyone for the decisions I've made because I am the person that has power over my life. If I want a different tomorrow, I have to have the self-discipline to make changes in today.

Self-discipline says I won't eat certain things. Self-discipline says I will do what I don't feel like doing. Self-discipline says I will do what needs to be done to have what I hope to have. Self-discipline is taking responsibility for my future and taking responsibility for my life.

Earlier this year I had a goal of losing twenty-five pounds, and I accomplished that goal by self-discipline. My new goal is to lose another twenty pounds and that will be accomplished by me exercising self-discipline and following my nutritional plan. I have another goal of writing this book, and part of writing this book is having the self-discipline to write every day and communicate what needs to be communicated and getting it out on paper. Every athlete will tell you that the difference between a player and a champion is the level of self-discipline in the off-season to work on your game, projects, and craft. When you live this way you will be ready so when opportunity presents itself, success is inevitable. Success happens when opportunity meets readiness. To be ready you have to have self-discipline. I can remember wanting to go to the parties while in college. There were parties every night. But I had to remain focused so that I could achieve my dream. When I was in high school I loved video games. I loved the challenge of trying to beat the game. There were times I spent hours trying to improve my score. My goal was to beat the game. Unfortunately, I had some other goals that also needed focused attention and dedication. I had to decide which goals I was going to work towards. I had to practice the self- discipline necessary to say no to somethings I wanted to do and say yes to somethings I needed to do. I had to practice self-discipline to achieve my goals. Self-discipline is necessary. Self-discipline is valuable. There are many that struggle with the time spent keeping up with social media. The challenge now is who can have the largest following. The question that we have to ask ourselves is how does this investment of time translate to some of our other goals that we may want to achieve in life. Then we are faced with the choice. Where are we going to invest?

Notes

What is my next move?

_____

_____

_____

_____

_____

_____

_____

_____

What specifically am I going to work on?

_____

_____

_____

_____

_____

_____

_____

_____

_____

Chapter 20: Thankful

Develop an attitude of gratitude, and give thanks for everything that
happens to you, knowing that every step forward is a step toward
achieving something bigger and better than your current situation.

—*Brian Tracy*

Thank·ful (adjective)

Expressing gratitude and relief

We must develop an attitude of gratitude and thankfulness to achieve success. Gratitude and thankfulness are the expressions of being grateful and appreciative for what you have, where you are, and what you have already accomplished. So many people get discouraged because they have not achieved their vision or they have not achieved a certain status in life. They allow these feelings of discontentment to rob them of the opportunity to be thankful for what they have already achieved. Many of us have a lot of things that we are proud of. We are grateful for the things that we have accomplished, things that we have achieved. We are to be thankful for those moments. We have to be grateful for the opportunity. We have to be thankful for the people who helped us along the way. Nobody can achieve anything of greatness unless there's a lot of people that are helping to accomplish that goal.

As students, we are to be thankful and grateful for those who come alongside and help in such a way that gives us the opportunity to express our greatness. I love sports. I especially love team sports. When we think about football, in order for the quarterback and the team to win, the line has to protect the quarterbacks, and the receiver must catch the ball. On the other side of the ball, the defense has to stop the other team from scoring. In order for all of us to be successful, I have to be thankful for your contribution. Everyone has something to contribute, everyone has something to give. Creating this attitude of thankfulness puts us in a position of success.

I am thankful for my wife. I am thankful for my children. I am thankful for my parents, and thankful for my siblings. I'm thankful for my immediate family and my extended family. I am thankful for my friends. I'm thankful for those who support me. I'm thankful to those who inspire me as well I'm thankful to my Savior Jesus Christ. I am thankful for my mentors. I am also thankful to my tutors. I can remember in college I needed to pass French to graduate. I struggled in the course. A foreign exchange student helped me with this course. Without her help, I would not have passed the class and may have had to take the course over again. I am thankful for the help I received, which then further motivated me to want to help others.

Notes

What is my next move?

_____

_____

_____

_____

_____

_____

_____

_____

What specifically am I going to work on?

_____

_____

_____

_____

_____

_____

_____

_____

_____

CHAPTER 21: UNBEATABLE

At the end of the day you gotta feel some way. So why not feel
unbeatable? Why not feel untouchable. —*Conor McGregor*

un·beat·a·ble adjective

not able to be defeated or exceeded in a contest or commercial
market.

Many people spend a lot of time trying to be like someone
else. They will try to wear what others wear, try to sing the way
they sing and try to act the way they act. Many people spend a lot
of time on Instagram, Facebook, and other social media platforms
such as YouTube trying to see what others do so, they can try to be
like them. One of the keys to being successful is that you identify
your uniqueness. You are unbeatable at being yourself. There is
nobody quite like you. There is nobody in the universe that has
your fingerprint, your DNA, your gifts, talent, or ability. No one
else feels your burdens, joys, sorrow, or pain. Nobody has your
story or experience. All of these things have come together to create

you as an unbeatable force at being yourself. Any successful person will tell you that the key to their success was just being themselves. I challenge you to spend time studying yourself discovering who you are and discovering why you're here. When you discover who you are, why you're here, and you match your passion to your pain, your purpose becomes revealed.

There was a story about a young man from my favorite book in the whole world. This young man's name was David. He was out taking care of his father's sheep as a teenager. His older brothers were in the military and they were at war. David's father sent him to the battle ground to take lunch for his brothers. When David got there the entire army was at a standstill because of a great champion fighter. The champion fighter challenged the army that David's brothers were fighting for. The military champion from the other side made a challenge to any of the men to fight him one on one, winner takes all. There were no takers from David's brothers 'army. So, David told the king that He would be willing to fight. They accepted, and got David suited with the best armor. David told them that he did not need the armor. He faced the giant with his weapons that he was comfortable with. David came out victorious because he chose to stick with what he was familiar with. He knew that He was unbeatable at being himself.

In my life, I spent a lot of time worrying about the opinions of people. I spent a lot of time worrying about what they thought, and worried about pleasing them. What I discovered was that the reason why I appeared to be unsuccessful in certain circles was because I was committed to excellence while others may have been committed to being average. Many people are not willing to pay the price or make the changes necessary to succeed. They preferred to remain comfortable with the present than embrace the possibility of a better future. When you discover not only who you are but that you are also unbeatable at being yourself, you become comfortable in your own skin. You also recognize that you already have found what others are searching for. As a result, you will no longer be driven by the opinions of other people. No longer will you allow yourself to be defined by the descriptions of others. You understand and accept that you are a person of purpose, a person of destiny, and a person who is here to accomplish something. You are a person of value.

Notes

What is my next move?

_____

_____

_____

_____

_____

_____

_____

_____

_____

What specifically am I going to work on?

_____

_____

_____

_____

_____

_____

_____

_____

_____

_____

Chapter 22: Vision

Vision

the ability to think about or plan the future with imagination or wisdom

"Where there is no vision, there is no hope." George Washington Carver

Vision is everything. What you see will determine what you will be. Vision is the ability to think about or plan your future with imagination and wisdom. You're able to Picture yourself in a desired future state. There are many athletes that visualize their success before the game or the race. They see themselves throwing the ball jump in the hoop getting out of the blocks fast.

Vision lives in the realm of imagination. Imagination is that place in your mind where you're able to visualize things that have not come to pass as yet. Imagination is so powerful because no matter what you're going through at the present moment you can have a picture of a better tomorrow. There are some of us who were born in situations that we had no control over. We didn't choose our parents, we didn't choose the skin color, we didn't choose our gender, we didn't choose what family we would belong to. But one beautiful thing about life is, how you start does not have to determine how you end. How are you and is entirely up to you. Depending upon the kind of life that you want to create the kind of life that you envision. It's very important to expose yourself to a number of successful people. As you associate yourself with them and look at their lives it enlarges your vision. You begin to dream a bigger dream, you begin to see bigger things. You begin to see yourself doing greater than what you're doing right now. What takes you from one level to another level is a vision. What takes you to another level of influence is vision. No matter where you are in life and no matter where what station you are a life It does not have to determine where are you ultimately end up in life. Vision is everything. Vision is what pulls you through those very depressing and dark moments. Dr. Martin Luther King Junior was a leader in the civil rights movement who had a vision and he phrased it this way, "I have a dream and the dream was that one day people would be judged not by the color of your skin but by the content of their character. The reason why that was a dream at that time was because that was not the current reality in society. He had a dream and a vision that everyone would rise to that level of integrity and moral clarity. Nelson Mandela stood up against apartheid in South Africa and gave up a number of years of his life because he believed that people could do better. Mother Theresa had a vision of taking care of the less fortunate and devoted her life to making that vision a reality.

I can remember when I was younger and I was in college and I would think about the idea of being married. I dreamt about going to buy furniture with my wife. I dreamt about having children and playing with them. And these were pictures that I had in my mind while I was still in college years before I met my wife and years before I had my first child. It was the picture of success, this picture of a family that drove some of the decisions that I made. I persevered in some of the difficult classes. I stayed up late at night studying because I wanted to be in a position to provide and realize my vision.

I can also remember as a little boy thinking about my family and specifically thinking about the kind of family that I was going to have, being a father and taking care of my children. Having fun playing with them, knowing that they were safe that they were provided for, that they had everything that they needed. I had that vision as a young man. And as an older person now I'm actually living what I saw and I'm living what I saw when I was a boy and I made decisions when I was young. I made a decision I was not going to have any children with somebody other than my wife and that was a vision that I had because there were so many other examples that I saw and did not want. I saw some of the complications that arose from having children prior to being married. Another vision that I had was that I was gonna have children with just one person and I'm living that vision right now. My children are the recipients of that vision, where all of my children share the same mother and same father and are reaping the benefits of that vision that I had as a boy. The vision was based on what I desired in the future and that impacted the decisions that I made because that vision was so powerful.

Everything you see around you started as a vision, everything you see around you started as an idea. There's somebody who said that I can make a chair because people need to sit down. They first had a vision in their mind and then they made that chair into a reality. There's somebody who said well I think we could have a table and so they looked at some trees and they had a vision that a table could come out of those trees. Somebody had a vision about shoes and they looked at some of the cows and some of the sheep and some of the alligators and said I think I can get some shoes out of these creatures. Everything starts with a vision.

You have great ideas. You have brilliant ideas. You have solutions to problems. You have answers to questions. You have innovations to create. All of these things begin in your mind. In your mind is where you have the imagination for the vision to create a better tomorrow to create some thing that solves a problem. Your vision is your key to your future. Your ability to see into the future your ability to see something better is what is key to your success. You have to picture it before you can have it, you have to see it before you can do it, you have to first finish it in your mind before you finish it in reality. This is the power of vision.

As you dream about your tomorrow and about where you want to be, and what you want to do, some of the questions that you need to ask yourselves: Where do I want to be in the next three years, where do I want to be in the next five years where do I want to be in the next 10 years? The answers to these questions will dictate how you conduct yourself, how you carry yourself, what you do and how you do it. Always remember vision is everything.

Notes

What is my next move?

_____

_____

_____

_____

_____

_____

_____

_____

What specifically am I going to work on?

_____

_____

_____

_____

_____

_____

_____

_____

_____

_____

Chapter 23: Winner

For me, winning isn't something that happens suddenly on the field when the whistle blows and the crowds roar. Winning is something that builds physically and mentally every day that you train and every night that you dream.

—*Emmitt Smith*

Win·ner (*noun*)

a person or thing that wins something.

Winning happens on the inside before it happens on the outside. A winning attitude is a disposition that corresponds with the vision of being successful. To be successful you must first perceive that success and agree with that success internally before you see it externally. There are many people who sabotage themselves by thinking that winning is something that just happens by accident. They believe that winning is only for certain groups. As a result, they fail to make the changes necessary to win. Winning happens because of intentional, deliberate, and disciplined life choices. Winning happens when there is an agreement between what we see internally, how we talk, and how we act. Everyone was designed to win in a specific area in life. It is then up to every individual to be their authentic selves. Everyone must be true to themselves. As a result, everyone must study himself. We must make it a point to study ourselves so that we can discover and uncover our hidden greatness. Then we can walk into our winning season that has been designed for every human on the face of this earth.

As a winner, I know that there are areas of my game that I need to improve on during the off-season so that I can add those elements into my overall game to improve myself as a player. This type of strategy is necessary for both sports and school and every other area of your life. To be a winner in life we have to have an attitude of improvement at all times, that there is always room for improvement, that there is always room for growth, and that there is always room to become better. Winning is the discipline to reject success for today for future success tomorrow.

I admire the New England Patriots. After losing the Super Bowl in 2008, they came back and won multiple Super Bowl Championships. They were a team that was committed to improving and winning. Many teams and people, after losing a particular battle, never get back to the championship form or the championship level. It is a winner's mindset to decide that even though I may have lost a battle, I may have lost the war, I may have lost the game, but it doesn't define my destiny. I am a winner. I was born a winner. I was born to dominate. I was born to be a champion in every area of my life. I have made the commitment to myself to press on towards this mark of excellence.

Notes

What is my next move?

_____

_____

_____

_____

_____

_____

_____

_____

What specifically am I going to work on?

_____

_____

_____

_____

_____

_____

_____

_____

_____

_____

CHAPTER 24: X-FACTOR

Being different is good; embrace it.

—Simon Cowell

X-fac·tor (noun)

a noteworthy special talent or quality.

There are plenty of luxury cars around, but the S-Type has that special X factor.

a variable in a given situation that could have the most significant impact on the outcome.

The young vote may turn out to be the X factor.

Everyone on earth has a gift, a talent, a unique quality that is God-given. This unique quality is your X-factor. It is a unique quality that gives you the ability to exercise dominion and authority in your sphere of expertise. As a student, I spent a lot of time watching people. I watched what people wore, what they said, and how they said it. I spent more time trying to keep up with what was going on in other people's lives that I did not appreciate what was going on in my life. I can remember one day in eighth grade, I was talking to a few friends and a teacher, Mr. Faulks, stopped me and called me over. He said, "young man don't you know you have an amazing voice?" Little did I know that later on in life I would become a speaker and a preacher, speaking all over the world. I did not discover and appreciate my unique quality until later in life. My gift of speaking has opened up doors all over the world.

Many people don't know this but I love super heroes. I love the story line of them going through some type of adversity that later leads to discovery. As a kid growing up, I loved Superman, and always wanted to fly. As I got older and was introduced to other superheroes, I think my favorite is now Black Panther. He has an X-Factor that separates him from all of the other heroes. He is one with one of the most powerful substances on planet earth.

The main pursuit in life for any person is the pursuit of self-discovery to discover your unique purpose. After this discovery the second most important pursuit is self-mastery. Once you discover your gift, it is now up to you to work on that gift so that you become the best at it. You work your gift so much that people are now willing to pay you for your gift. People will begin to appreciate your value and contribution, and this is your key to success.

Notes

What is my next move?

_____

_____

_____

_____

_____

_____

_____

_____

_____

What specifically am I going to work on?

_____

_____

_____

_____

_____

_____

_____

_____

_____

_____

Dr. Rudolph A. Moseley, Jr.

CHAPTER 25: YOUR TRUE VALUE

Your time is way too valuable to be wasting on people that can't accept who you are.

—*Turcois Ominek*

Val·ue (*noun*)

the regard that something is held to deserve; the importance, worth, or usefulness of something.

Knowing your true value begins with believing in yourself. Believing in yourself and knowing your true worth is essential for you to become successful in life. If you don't value yourself, nobody else will. If you don't value your contribution, nobody else will. If you don't think that you are worth something, nobody else will. Knowing your true value is essential for you to understand that you are a problem solver. In life, the size problem you solve will determine the kind of fee you will be able to command.

Knowing how important and needed you are in the world is essential to your true value.

We are paid based on the problems that we solve, and in order for you to be successful and valuable to somebody, you have to know what you're bringing to the table - who you were created to help. A gift is meaningful depending upon how skilled you are at giving your gift away. A doctor solves medical problems. A lawyer solves legal problems. Teachers solve education problems. Folks who work at the more common jobs get paid minimum wage because their contribution is not deemed essential. Your gift will give you the ability to determine how high you can go in your field. Knowing your true value, knowing that you are valuable will give you the ability to command whatever price because people respect you and believe that you can solve their problem.

I can remember growing up and thinking about the idea of becoming a doctor. I thought about how many years of school I was going to have to commit to. But when I thought about it some more, I recognized that to solve complex problems you may have to study so that you have the knowledge to solve those types of problems. I then thought to myself that when it comes to STEM fields the reason why these jobs seem to pay higher than other jobs is because of the schooling and years of study and practice required to solve these types of problems. I have a degree in biology and a minor in chemistry. I have a masters degree in education and a doctoral degree in education. I have my teaching license in biology, and general science. I have a school administrator's license and a superintendent license. I am also an ordained minister, a husband and a father. With all of these opportunities and experiences in life what I have noticed is that the bigger the required solution, the bigger the check. Having the ability to inspire people to become their best is my true value. All of the achievements I have made were really not for me but for the people I speak to that struggled like I did. So that I could let them know that it is possible. Despite your struggles and mistakes, there is success around the corner.

You are a problem solver. Your life is a gift and you are carrying solutions to the problems in the world.

Notes

What is my next move?

_____

_____

_____

_____

_____

_____

_____

_____

What specifically am I going to work on?

_____

_____

_____

_____

_____

_____

_____

_____

_____

_____

CHAPTER 26: ZEAL

Live your truth. Express your love. Share your enthusiasm. Take action towards your dreams. Walk your talk. Dance and sing to your music. Embrace your blessings. Make today worth remembering. —Steve Maraboli

Zeal (*noun*)

great energy or enthusiasm in pursuit of a cause or an objective.

Zeal speaks of energy. It speaks of enthusiasm and passion. It speaks of intentionality. It speaks of being decisive. Zeal is necessary to step into the realm of success. You are not going to achieve anything of greatness or significance without being enthusiastic and having the energy to do so. Hustle wins. Hustle will always beat out talent any day.

Once there were two aspiring athletes who tried out for their high school basketball team. At the tryouts, it was obvious that one guy was more talented than the other. When it came time for the coach to decide, he chose the player that was not as talented but had more hustle. When asked why he made the decision, he explained that he selected the guy with more hustle because he knew what he was going to get every game. With the more talented player, you could not plan because you did not know who was going to show up. There are many talented people who are broke. They lack the hustle to get things done. Zeal speaks of why, we do what we do. What are the reasons why we want to accomplish the goals? What are the reasons we want to fulfill our dreams? What are the reasons why we sacrifice, the reasons why we discipline ourselves? Zeal actually puts us in a position so that we can accomplish the dreams that we desire to accomplish.

When I went off to college, there were many people in my family that were extremely proud. I was not the first male in my family to go to college. However I did become the first boy to have a Masters and a Doctoral degree in my entire family. I can remember every time I would go home for vacation and I would see all of my cousins and my sisters and brothers who were so proud that I was in school. Their belief in me fueled my zeal to push myself. I did not want to disappoint anyone. I had a zeal to complete what I started. I wanted to make my family proud.

It's hard to have zeal for something that we don't believe in. So it's essential for us to be true to who we are. We must be authentic and sincere about our beliefs so that we can run with confidence and with patience towards the vision and destiny and with enthusiasm at the end of our goal. In my life, I have been passionate about many things. However, nothing compares to the zeal I had to complete this book. There are things in this book that I wish someone had told me. There are principles in this book that had I known earlier in life I would have gotten to where I am faster.

As you have read/reviewed these principles, understand that they require daily practice, and that learning/committing them to memory and habitual implementation will help in achieving your desired level of success. I hope you discover your why early so that you can devote the remainder of your life to your purpose. You have a bright future. I believe in you. You have greatness on the inside and you are capable of discovering it and bringing it out. Use this Playbook as your guide. Believe it today and you will be successful in life.

Notes

What is my next move?

_____

_____

_____

_____

_____

_____

_____

_____

What specifically am I going to work on?

_____

_____

_____

_____

_____

_____

_____

_____

_____

CPSIA information can be obtained
at www.ICGtesting.com
Printed in the USA
BVHW031914100621
609295BV00013B/117